Axel Jörn

Dynamic capabilities at IBM

Anchor Academic
Publishing

Jörn, Axel: Dynamic capabilities at IBM, Hamburg, Anchor Academic Publishing 2016

Buch-ISBN: 978-3-96067-008-7
PDF-eBook-ISBN: 978-3-96067-508-2
Druck/Herstellung: Anchor Academic Publishing, Hamburg, 2016

Bibliografische Information der Deutschen Nationalbibliothek:
Die Deutsche Nationalbibliothek verzeichnet diese Publikation in der Deutschen Nationalbibliografie; detaillierte bibliografische Daten sind im Internet über http://dnb.d-nb.de abrufbar.

Bibliographical Information of the German National Library:
The German National Library lists this publication in the German National Bibliography. Detailed bibliographic data can be found at: http://dnb.d-nb.de

All rights reserved. This publication may not be reproduced, stored in a retrieval system or transmitted, in any form or by any means, electronic, mechanical, photocopying, recording or otherwise, without the prior permission of the publishers.

Das Werk einschließlich aller seiner Teile ist urheberrechtlich geschützt. Jede Verwertung außerhalb der Grenzen des Urheberrechtsgesetzes ist ohne Zustimmung des Verlages unzulässig und strafbar. Dies gilt insbesondere für Vervielfältigungen, Übersetzungen, Mikroverfilmungen und die Einspeicherung und Bearbeitung in elektronischen Systemen.

Die Wiedergabe von Gebrauchsnamen, Handelsnamen, Warenbezeichnungen usw. in diesem Werk berechtigt auch ohne besondere Kennzeichnung nicht zu der Annahme, dass solche Namen im Sinne der Warenzeichen- und Markenschutz-Gesetzgebung als frei zu betrachten wären und daher von jedermann benutzt werden dürften.

Die Informationen in diesem Werk wurden mit Sorgfalt erarbeitet. Dennoch können Fehler nicht vollständig ausgeschlossen werden und die Diplomica Verlag GmbH, die Autoren oder Übersetzer übernehmen keine juristische Verantwortung oder irgendeine Haftung für evtl. verbliebene fehlerhafte Angaben und deren Folgen.

Alle Rechte vorbehalten

© Anchor Academic Publishing, Imprint der Diplomica Verlag GmbH
Hermannstal 119k, 22119 Hamburg
http://www.diplomica-verlag.de, Hamburg 2016
Printed in Germany

Contents

List of figures 9

List of tables 9

List of abbreviations 9

1 Introduction 11
    1.1 Task of the assignment 11
    1.2 Importance of Change 11
        1.2.1 Technological Advancements 12
        1.2.2 Crisis Management 12
        1.2.3 Customer Needs 13
        1.2.4 External Factors 13
        1.2.5 Organizational Culture 13
        1.2.6 The Economy 13
        1.2.7 Growth Opportunities 14
        1.2.8 Challenging the Status Quo 14
        1.2.9 Information about IBM 14
    1.3 Transition of IBM 15
        1.3.1 IBMs Engines of Growth 16

2 Theoretical basis of dynamic capabilities and strategic management 18
    2.1 Definition of dynamic capabilities and innovation 19
    2.2 Roots of the dynamic capabilities perspective 19
    2.3 Aspects of dynamic capabilities 21
        2.3.1 Adaptive capabilities 21
        2.3.2 Absorptive capabilities 21
        2.3.3 Innovative capabilities 22
    2.4 Relationship to organisational variables 23
    2.5 Methods to foster dynamic capabilities 25
        2.5.1 Promoting Entrepreneurship 25
        2.5.2 Organisational Ambidexterity 26
        2.5.3 Lobbyism and Acquire hiring 27

3 Analyses of the dynamic capabilities within IBM 28
3.1 The IBM Business Leadership Model 29
3.1.1 Strategy 30
3.1.2 Execution 30
3.2 IBM's Dynamic capabilities 31
3.2.1 Sensing new opportunities 31
3.2.2 Seizing new opportunities 32
3.3 Cultural change 34
3.4 The success in concrete results and figures 35
4 Conclusion 39
4.1 Relationship to organisational variables 39
4.2 The three main aspects of dynamic capabilities 40
4.3 Organisational Ambidexterity 40
4.4 Promoting Entrepreneurship 41
4.5 Lobbyism and Acquire hiring 42
4.6 Recommendation 42

List of appendices 43

List of references 44

List of internet references 45

Appendix 1: ITM Checklist 47

List of figures

Figure 1: Sales of IBM worldwide from Q2 2009 to Q4 2014 (in billions of US dollars) 15
Figure 2: IBM strategic imperative revenue mix 17
Figure 3: Origins of the dynamic capabilities perspective 20
Figure 4: Organisational relationships and dynamic capabilities 24
Figure 5: The three types of dynamic capabilities and the RBV linked to environments 25
Figure 6: Ten Characteristics to foster Ambidexterity in organisations 27
Figure 7: The IBM Business Leadership Model 29
Figure 8: IBM Segment pretax income 37
Figure 9: EBO Revenue as a Percent of Total IBM Revenue 41

List of tables

Table 1: Comparison of adaptors referring to aspects of absorptive capabilities 22
Table 2: Sensing new opportunities within the IBM Business Leadership Model 32

List of abbreviations

IBM	International Business Machines
CTR	Computing-Tabulating-Recording
RBV	Resource Based View
SWOT	Strength weaknesses, opportunities and threats
MBV	Market Bases View
KBV	Knowledge Based View
CEO	Chef Executive Officer
EBO	Emerging Business Opportunities
SLF	Strategic Leadership Forum

1 Introduction

1.1 Task of the assignment

This assignment with the topic "Dynamic capabilities at International Business Machines (IBM)" was created in the second semester "Strategic Corporate Management" module to obtain the „Master of Business Administration". This assignment starts with an introduction of the company IBM. In the second part the theoretical basis for dynamic capabilities is described. The third part explains the practical execution of the dynamic capabilities within IBM. Finally this assignment draws a conclusion and gives a recommendation for future research.

1.2 Importance of Change

Already Charles Darwin's wisdom about the survival of the fittest is implying the importance of the ability to change.

> *"It is not the strongest of the species that survive, nor the most intelligent,*
> *but the one that is most responsive to change."*

This insight is also valid in business. A study of U.S. manufacturing firms in the 20th century reported that only 28 of the initial 266 companies remained over the period from 1917 to 1997. The selection across three major time periods shows that 49% of the firms appear only once, and then disappear, suggesting that most firms do not adapt. A study of the life expectancy of firms has uncovered that in 1935, the average expectancy was 90 years. By 1975, that number had fallen to 30 years, and in 2005 it was projected to be only 15 years. That means, being successful at one point in time is not an assurance of sustainability and continued survival. Similarly, a study with 6772 firms across 40 industries over 25 years showed only a small minority exhibited greater economic performance. Famous examples are firms such as Polaroid, PanAm, Sears, and Bethlehem Steel who didn't managed to adapt to changing environments.[1]

On the other hand there are positive examples of firms that began in an industry or technology different from the one they compete in today like GKN, a 245 year-old aero-space materials

---

[1] Rf.: O'Reilly III, C.A. (2007), page 3-4

and auto parts maker, that arose as a coal mining company, or the more than 100 year old Harris Corporation, a high tech electronics firm that originated manufacturing printing presses. The aviation supplier Goodrich was founded in 1870 as a manufacturer of conveyor belts and fire hose.[2] These companies were able to keep up with the time.

In modern business, things like technologies markets, ideas and inventions change at an exponential rate. There has never been a more important time to ensure change efforts intended to maintain growth, expansion and morale. Change is important for any organization because, without change, businesses would likely lose its competitive edge and fail to meet the need of loyal customers and the base to growth. Almost every company is facing some kind of change implementation because of competitive pressures, economic challenges, skill shortages, a necessity to grow and expand, or the need for a culture change.[3]

1.2.1 Technological Advancements

Technology is considered as the engine of growth in today's world. Perhaps the greatest challenge for contemporary organizations is the acquisition and integration of technology in its strategy, structure and process.[4] Change is important in coping with emerging technological advancements in the society. Transforming the business in line with new technologies helps it to edge out its competitors, thanks to increased productivity. Change that results from the adoption of new technology is common in most organizations and while it can be disruptive at first, ultimately the change tends to increase productivity and service. Incorporating change in line with technology helps the development of new procedures for carrying out various needed tasks.[5]

1.2.2 Crisis Management

Change becomes a necessity when an organization finds itself in a crisis. It helps it rectify some of its processes or activities that may have become ineffective. Initiating changes to discard these processes assists the organization to withstand turbulent times. Furthermore, changes spare the firm from extra expenses of sustaining the ineffectual processes. The understanding of change is important in combating challenges such as fears of lay-offs, incompatible corporate cultures and increased turnover -- which often arise from acquisitions and mergers.

---

[2] ibid, page 5
[3] Rf.: KenBlanchard (2010), page 44
[4] Rf.: Zeepedia (2015): Change Management.
[5] Rf.: Everydaylife (2015): GlobalPost.

1.2.3 Customer Needs

As the world evolves, customer needs are changing constantly. That results in demands for new types of products and services, and opening up new areas of opportunity for companies to meet those needs.

1.2.4 External Factors

Change helps organizations to cope with globalization, which can be a threat or an opportunity. Globalization has made it possible for companies to produce goods and services at lower costs in some areas than in others. In coping with globalization, businesses need to understand the cultural and regional differences in various markets. Such an understanding equips them with the knowledge to develop strategies for these markets.

1.2.5 Organizational Culture

Many companies initiate change to improve their organizational culture. Changing the organizational culture, which could include basic beliefs, values, feelings, and internal and external relationships, can improve its efficiency and productivity. Effective organizational culture also attracts new customers, increases customer satisfaction, reduces costs of operations and increases worker retention.[6]

1.2.6 The Economy

The Economy can impact organizations in both positive and negative ways and both can be stressful. A strong economy and increasing demand for products and services will mean that companies must consider expansion that might involve the addition of staff and new facilities. These changes offer opportunities for staff, but also represent new challenges. A weak economy can create even more problems as companies find themselves needing to make difficult decisions that can impact employees' salaries and benefits and even threaten their jobs. The ability to manage both ends of the spectrum is critical for organizations that want to maintain a strong brand and strong relationships with customers as well as employees.

---

[6] Rf.: Everydaylife (2015): GlobalPost.

1.2.7 Growth Opportunities

Change is important in organizations to allow employees to learn new skills, explore new opportunities and exercise their creativity in ways that ultimately benefit the organization through new ideas and increased commitment.

1.2.8 Challenging the Status Quo

Simply asking the question "Why?" can lead to new ideas and new innovations that can directly impact the core business of a company. Organizations benefit from change that results in new ways of looking at customer needs, new ways of delivering customer service, new ways of strengthening customer interactions and new products that might attract new markets. New employees joining an organization are especially valuable because they can often point to areas of opportunity for improvement that those who have been long involved in the company might have overlooked. But even existing employees should be encouraged to question why things are done a certain way and look for new ways to get work done faster, better and with higher levels of quality and service.[7]

1.2.9 Information about IBM

On June 16, 1911, IBM began operation as the Computing-Tabulating-Recording (CTR)-Company. At this time the New York City-based Company had around 1,300 employees. It manufactured and sold machinery ranging from commercial scales and industrial time recorders to meat and cheese slicers, along with tabulators and punched cards. On February 14, 1924, CTR was renamed the International Business Machines Corporation (IBM), citing the need to align its name with the growth and extension of its activities.[8]

IBM has constantly evolved since its inception. Over the past decade, it has steadily shifted its business mix by exiting commoditizing businesses such as PCs, hard disk drives and Memories and focusing on higher-value, more profitable businesses such as business intelligence, data analytics, business continuity, security, cloud computing, virtualization and green solutions.[9]

Today, IBM is an American multinational computer technology and consulting corporation, with headquarters in Armonk, New York. IBM manufactures and markets computer hardware

---

[7] Rf.: Chron (2015): Change in Organizations.
[8] Rf.: TheAtlantic (2011): IBM's First 100 Years
[9] Rf.: IBM Annual Report (2008), page 2-4

and software, and offers infrastructure, hosting and consulting services in areas ranging from mainframe computers to nanotechnology. In 2014, IBM had total revenue of USD 92.793 billion with a net income of USD 12.023 billion. IBM operates in more than 170 countries and has more than 379,000 employees worldwide.[10] In November 2014, Forbes ranked IBM No. 5 the world most valuable brand.[11]

1.3 Transition of IBM

Hardware sales continued their slide in the first quarter 2015 as IBM exited the commodity server business and focused instead on its more profitable Unix and mainframe computers. IBM reported on April 20, 2015 that sales at its hardware group totalled $1.7 billion for the first quarter of 2015, down from $2.4 billion during the same period last year. Most of the drop came from IBM's sale last year of its commodity server business to Lenovo Group Ltd.

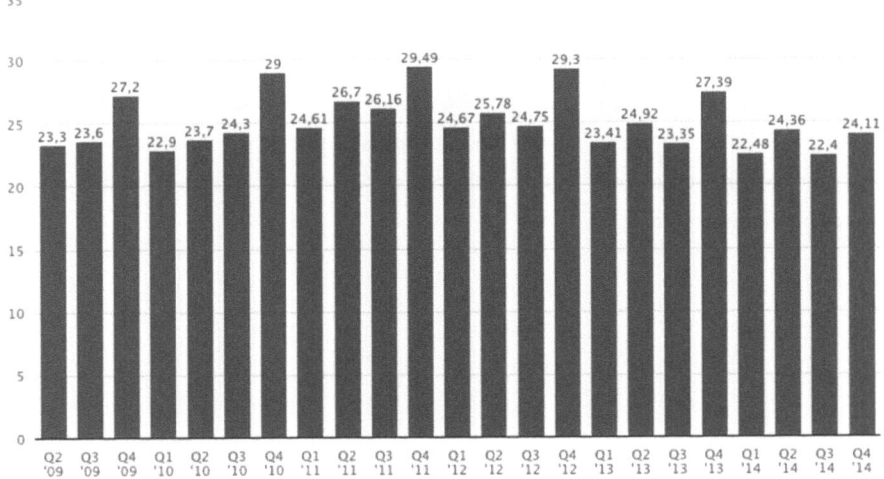

Figure 1: Sales of IBM worldwide from Q2 2009 to Q4 2014 (in billions of US dollars)[12]

Revenue dropped to $19.59 billion from $22.24 billion as a surging U.S. dollar compounded the impact of shrinking hardware sales. It was the company's 12th straight quarter of year-on-

---

[10] Rf.: IBM Annual Report (2014), page 73-74
[11] Rf.: Forbes (2014): Powerful Brands
[12] Rf.: Statista (2015)

year declines. Revenue was flat from a year earlier excluding currency changes and divested businesses.[13] IBM had a relatively poor year in terms of revenue in 2014, but this did not prevent the company from investing heavily in R&D. IBM invested more than $6.3 billion in R&D in fiscal 2013, one of the highest figures among all companies worldwide.[14]

IBM is now in the midst of a massive structural reorganization to make it a serious player in the cloud. It has shifted its focus onto software, letting hardware take the back seat. In December 2014 IBM announced it was partnering with Apple to launch 10 IBM Mobile First for iOS apps. The apps range in capabilities to benefit governments as well as businesses in the banking, retail, insurance, financial services, telecom, and airline industries. In mid-January 2015, IBM unveiled the z13 mainframe, which it calls the most powerful and secure system ever built. The new system's scalability and reliability make it "the ideal private or hybrid cloud architecture," IBM stated. In fact, it can run up to 8,000 virtual servers. Restructuring clearly hasn't slowed down innovation at IBM. In 2014 IBM was the global leader for innovations for the 22nd consecutive year, with 7,534 patents.[15]

1.3.1 IBMs Engines of Growth

IBM pursues a model of high-value innovation, rather than commodity technology, products and services. IBMs commitment to this model compels them to reinvent businesses continually, grow new ones organically and through acquisitions, and occasionally divest businesses that do not fit our profile.

---

[13] Rf.: WSJ (2015): IBM
[14] Rf.: 247wallst (2015)
[15] Rf.: CC (2015), page 11

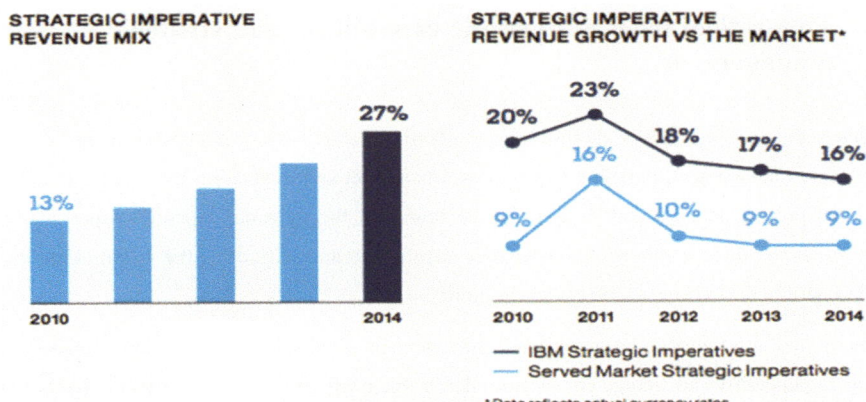

Figure 2: IBM strategic imperative revenue mix[16]

The strategic imperatives became a significant part of IBM. Together, cloud, analytics, mobile, social and security generated $25 billion of revenue in 2014, growing by 16 percent. Five years ago, these businesses represented just 13 percent of IBMs revenue. Today, that has risen to 27 percent of IBM's revenue. IBM generated more than 3,000 patents in these areas in 2014 and remains differentiated in their ability to integrate these technologies with their clients' core business processes, data and systems.[17]

Billionaire investor Warren Buffett says he remains confident in IBM's future and he believes that IBM will be making more money ten years from now than it does today. He thinks IBM will fare well in cloud computing and corporate services because of the level of security it offers with its products.[18] The trust of such big investor as Warren Buffett in IBMs future shows that IBM is on the right way to stay competitive in the most dynamic, fast-changing industries in the world.

The reorganisations, new products, patents and adaptations to the tremendous changes in the IT Environment are a strong indicator for the sound dynamic capabilities of IBM. But what are they precisely? In the next part the theoretical basics of the dynamic capability perspective is given whereas the practical part describes the dynamic capabilities specifically for IBM.

---

[16] Rf.: IBM Annual Report (2014), page 5
[17] ibid, page 4
[18] Rf.: Finance Yahoo (2015)

2 Theoretical basis of dynamic capabilities and strategic management

This section gives first a definition and shortly pictures the interdependencies between strategic management, dynamic capabilities, innovation and innovation-management and the related project management. It pictures the source of the dynamic capabilities perspective, describes the three components of dynamic capabilities and introduces the different methods and instruments to drive a strategy into action.

There are four frameworks in strategic management. Firstly, porters five force analyses in which competitive advantage comes from defensible positions against competitors like strong entry barriers. Second is the resource based view (RBV) of strategy where advantage is derived from difficult to imitate assets such as economies of scale or a dominant brand. The third approach is to emphasize a strategic conflict approach using the tools of game theory to outsmart a company's rivals. Recently the forth tactic of "dynamic capabilities" as feature in the field of strategic management became more popular. Whereas the first three methods are more static (develop a positional advantage and defend it) dynamic capabilities focus to the need for organizations to change actively and compete in both developing and established businesses.[19] Closely related to the dynamic capability discussion is the question about the organizational design and ambidexterity, the ability of a firm to simultaneously explore and exploit, which facilitates a firm to adapt over time.[20] Exploitation is characterised by increasing productivity, efficiency, certainty, control and variance reduction. Exploration is about autonomy, innovation, search, embracing variation and discovery.[21]

Apart from these major frameworks there are other strategic approaches such as Mc Kinsey's product-market-matrix, SWOT-analyses, market-based-view (MBV) & knowledge-based-view (KBV), Six- und Lean-Sigma.[22]

---

[19] Rf.: Dutta, S. (2012), page 82-83
[20] Rf.: O'Reilly III, C.A. (2007), page 2
[21] ibid, page 10
[22] Rf.: Dahm, M. H. (2007), page 15-24

2.1 Definition of dynamic capabilities and innovation

Dynamic can be understood in the same way as it is in mathematics, as a parameter dependent on the speed of a change. Hence, the dimension of a change (amplitude) and how often a change accrues (frequency). Capability is the organisational ability to change something and needs to be distinguished from the word "capacity" which addresses resources (finance, human and time) that are needed to fulfil a certain activity. Capability can be summarised as the ways in which an organisation may arrange its assets successfully.[23]

In literature one can find several definitions and diverse understandings of dynamic capabilities, but the definition from Professor David J. Teece and his colleagues (Gary Pisano and Amy Shuen) seemed to be most respected. He refined his definition from "The subset of the competences and capabilities that allow the firm to create new products and processes and respond to changing market circumstances" in 1994 to "Dynamic capabilities can be disaggregated into the capacity to **sense** and shape opportunities and threats, to **seize** opportunities, and to maintain competitiveness through enhancing, combining, protecting, and, when necessary, **reconfiguring** the business enterprise's intangible and tangible assets" in 2007.[24]

Teece is characterising all enterprises as successful that are able to react on time on market changes to achieve or maintain a competitive advantage. That means companies that bring fast and flexible product innovations and have a management in place that appropriately steers, allocates and coordinates internal and external resources. "This is to say, the firm's ability to integrate, build, and reconfigure internal and external competences to address rapidly changing environments."[25]

2.2 Roots of the dynamic capabilities perspective

In literature one can find primarily five sources of the dynamic capabilities perspective. These are the resource based view, core competences, capability based view, knowledge based view and organisational-capabilities.

- The resource-based-view understands an organisation as a unit of resources to what it has direct or indirect access to.

---

[23] Rf.: Hutterer, P. (2013), page 182
[24] Rieser, M. (2014), page 23
[25] Rf.: Hutterer, P. (2013), page 196

- Core-competences can be understood as a streamlined combination of various resources and skills that differentiate a firm in the marketplace.
- The capability-based-view is developed from the resource based view in the sense that it considers also a special type of resources —exactly, an firm specific resource whose purpose is to improve or even facilitate the efficiency or productivity of the other resources controlled by the firm (managerial skill).
- The knowledge-based-view is a wider perspective of the resource-based-view and puts knowledge to the centre of gravity of competitive advantage. In this viewpoint the organisation is not just only a unit of resources but a social establishment of individuals who interact on common convictions and ideologies.
- Organisational capabilities are complex interactions, coordination and problem solving technics which are based on dedicated knowledge groups in a long term development process. These technics and interaction can develop to organisational routines, methodologies and best practice.[26] The project management institute (PMI) summarises that to "organisational process assets".[27]

The following image shows constrains of the five roots of the dynamic capabilities perspective.

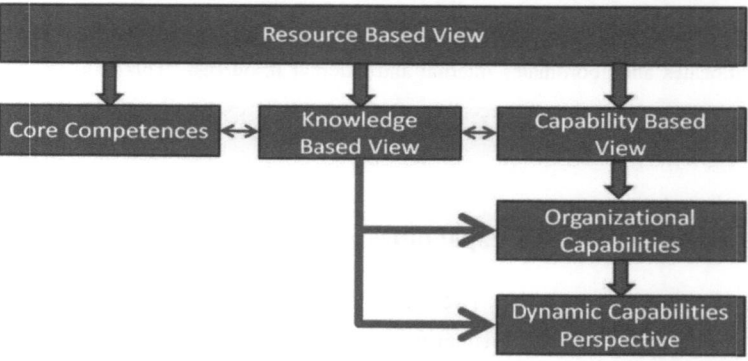

Figure 3: Origins of the dynamic capabilities perspective[28]

---

[26] ibid, page 183-189
[27] ibid, page 33
[28] ibid, page 195

2.3 Aspects of dynamic capabilities

There are three main components of dynamic capabilities. These are adaptive-, absorptive- and innovative capabilities.

2.3.1 Adaptive capabilities

"Adaptive capability is defined as a firm's ability to identify and capitalise on emerging market opportunities. This type of 'balancing' act is brought to a strategic level and linked to the resource perspective: adaptive capability is manifested through strategic flexibility - the inherent flexibility of the resources available to the firm and the flexibility in applying these resources."[29] Adaptability can be measured considering the following talents:

- Adapt a company's product or market scope to respond to external opportunities
- Scan the market, monitor customers and competitors and allocate resources to marketing activities
- Respond quickly to changing market conditions
- Encouraged people to challenge outmoded traditions and practices

Thus adaptive capabilities can be developed by the evolution of organisational structures.[30]

2.3.2 Absorptive capabilities

To be absorptive means to recognize the value of new and external information, to assimilate them, and apply them to commercial products or services. It is the ability to evaluate and utilize outside knowledge. The higher absorptive capability the stronger the ability of learning from partners, integrating external information and transforming it into firm knowledge. Firms can be more efficacious or less effective adaptors.[31] Absorptive capabilities can be acknowledged via the following characteristics:

---

[29] Wang, C. (2007), page 13-14
[30] Rf.: Wang, C. (2007), page 14
[31] ibid, page 15

More efficacious adaptors	Less efficacious adaptors
Demonstrate long-term commitment of resources in the face of uncertainty	Short-term limited commitment and reversed at the first sign of failure
Learn from various partners and own research and experience and develop first-hand knowledge of the new technology	Competitive imitation and second-hand knowledge
Thoroughly analyse the latest technologies and share information within multidisciplinary teams	Superficial analysis and functional structure
Develop and utilise complementary technologies	No complementary technologies used
Possess a high level of knowledge and skills in areas relevant to applying the new technology	

Table 1: Comparison of adaptors referring to aspects of absorptive capabilities[32]

2.3.3 Innovative capabilities

Innovation capability is the ability to develop new products, services, processes, methods of production, sources of supply, organisational forms and/or markets, through aligning strategic innovative orientation with innovative behaviours. Currently it is difficult to measure organisational innovative capabilities effectively, even though there are indicators defined. These indicators are: strategic-innovative-orientation and behavioural-, process-, product- and market-innovativeness.[33]

As innovation is the crucial point in this definition it can be stated that "dynamic capabilities" are not just aspects of strategic management but also to the scientific field of innovation management and furthermore to project management. Innovation means „something new" or „renew" and needs to be differentiated from the word invention. The invention is delineating an idea or a flash of inspiration and with that the first and creative step of the whole innovation process whereas the innovation is designating the development of an invention to a mature and "ready for the market" solution. An idea is the essential part of each innovation yet she is almost useless without a proper practice context or adequate implementation.[34] This implementation can be understood in turn as the stimulation of dynamic capabilities which can be organised or frosted with project management methods, tools and techniques.

"Projects are ubiquitous. They are everywhere, and everybody does them. Projects are the driving force for many organizations in most industries. Projects can be looked upon as the change efforts of society, and the pace of change has been increasing. Therefore, effectively

---
[32] ibid, page 15-16
[33] ibid, page 17
[34] Rf.: Amberg, M. (2010), page 111-112

and efficiently managing change efforts are the only way organizations can survive and grow in this modern world."[35]

An alternative nonetheless comparable interpretation of the literature regarding dynamic capabilities from Aimilia Protogerou has led to the identification of three processes as core elements of the dynamic capabilities concept: coordinating/integrating, learning, and strategic competitive response processes.[36]

2.4 Relationship to organisational variables

Dynamic capabilities are influenced or dependent via several relationships from different conditions. There a numerous of empirical studies which can be looked up in (Wang, C./Ahmed, P. (2007): Dynamic capabilities: A Review and Research Agenda) and that has originated the following constraints between dynamic capabilities and:

- Market dynamism: the more dynamic a market environment, the stronger the drive of an organisation to exhibit dynamic capabilities. (Link P1)
- Firms Strategy: The higher dynamic capabilities a firm demonstrates, the more likely it will build particular capabilities over the time; the focus on developing particular capabilities is dictated by the firm's overall business strategy. (Link P2) [37]
- Long term performance: "Dynamic capabilities are conductive to long-term firm performance, but the relationship is an indirect one mediated by capability development that, in turn, is mediated by firm strategy (Link P2); dynamic capabilities are more likely to lead to better firm performance when particular capabilities are developed in line with the firm's strategic choice." (Link P3)[38]

The next figure is showing the organisational variables with focus on dynamic capabilities and distinguishes between direct and indirect relationships.

---

[35] Dinsmore, P.C., page 1
[36] Rf.: Protogerou, A. (2011), page 619
[37] Rf.: Wang, C. (2007), page 20-23
[38] Wang, C. (2007), page 24

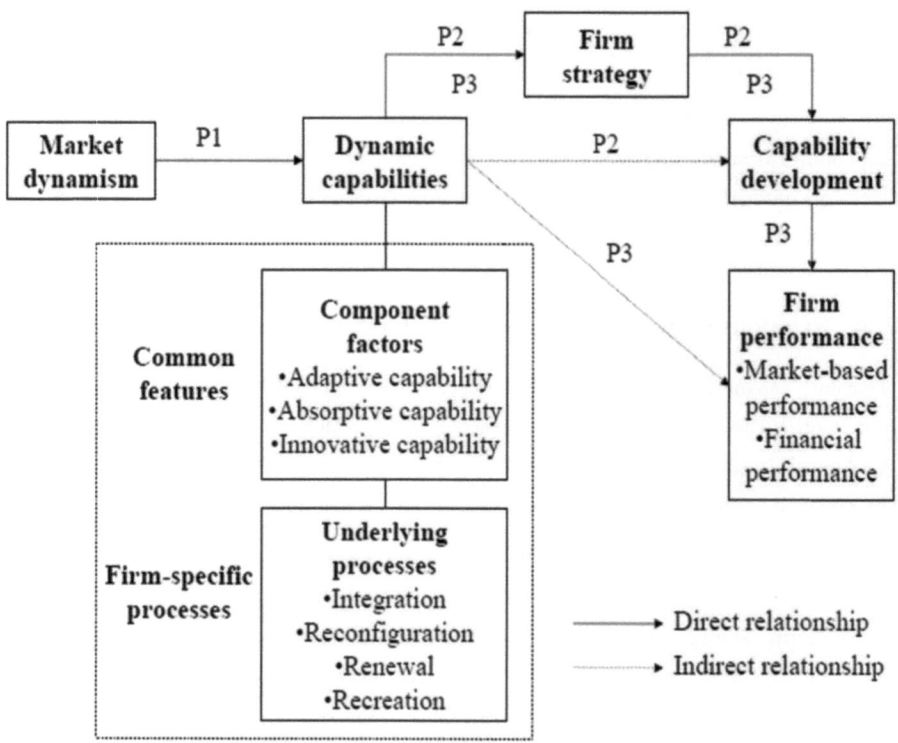

Figure 4: Organisational relationships and dynamic capabilities[39]

Another scientific research decomposes dynamic capabilities into three different types: incremental dynamic capabilities, renewable dynamic capabilities and regenerative dynamic capabilities.[40] To make it short, the figure on the next page shows there relationships, there organisational position and there reference to the RBV within the different types of environments.

---

[39] ibid, page 39
[40] Rf.: Ambrosini, V. (2009), page 12

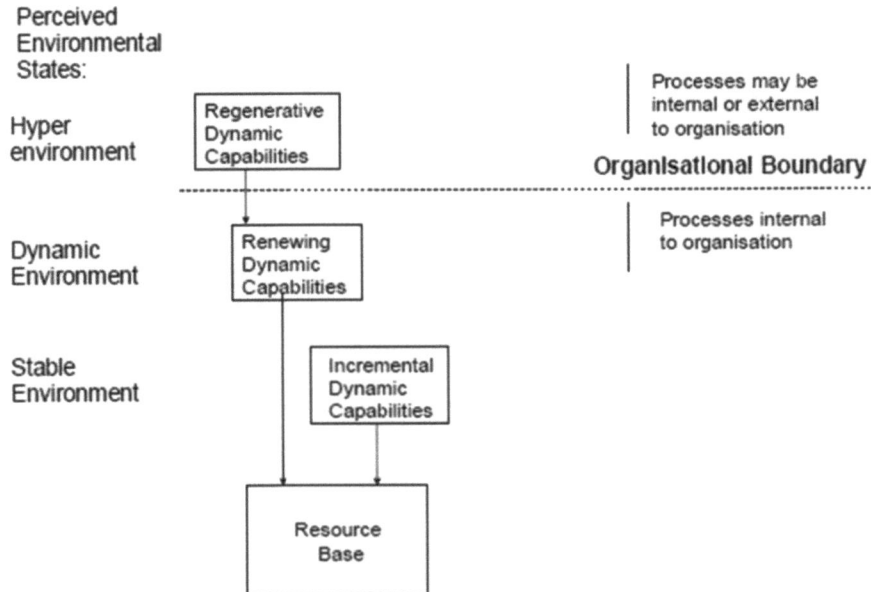

Figure 5: The three types of dynamic capabilities and the RBV linked to environments[41]

2.5 Methods to foster dynamic capabilities

These paragraphs represent the bridge between theory and practice and shortly introduce techniques and methods to foster or utilise dynamic capabilities.

2.5.1 Promoting Entrepreneurship

Entrepreneurship can be encouraged by creating different operating companies within a big group/concern. A good example is Jonson & Jonson (consumer products, pharmaceuticals, and professional medical products) which has over 150 separate corporations that constantly scan the surrounding for new market opportunities. This scanning (sensing) is one attribute of dynamic capabilities. ABB (power plants, electrical equipment, transportation systems and environmental controls) is divided into around 5000 profit centres with an average size of 50 people in each. These centres function like small businesses and act independently. L&T is an Indian company in the field of engineering and construction projects; heavy engineering;

---

[41] ibid, page 40

construction; electrical and electronics; machinery and industrial products; IT and financial services spread their portfolio across twelve operating companies between five and six independent divisions. This represents around 100 companies under one roof.[42]

Beside the organisational circumstances it is important to generate an open and experimental working atmosphere to facilitate an exchange of ideas and views across the organisation thereby endorsing entrepreneurship. Notwithstanding the position in an organisation employees have space for diversity of opinions and point of views. A higher sophisticated approach is the IBM Business Leadership Model. IBM is supporting open-source software by putting IBM intellectual property in the public. They offer technical services, in which IBM technical experts help other companies to design products and services. In this way IBM not just sense opportunities but as well sizes them.[43]

2.5.2 Organisational Ambidexterity

As already mentioned above ambidexterity is one aspect of dynamic capabilities. With respect to organisational ambidexterity, dynamic capabilities can be understood as a set of actions (or routines) taken by the management that enables an enterprise to identify opportunities and threats and reconfigure assets (people, organizational architectures, and resources) to react to these. "The following five senior leader attributes or activities are essential for organisational ambidexterity.

- A clear strategic intent that justifies the importance of the ambidextrous for future survival and provides intellectual engagement.
- Overarching vision and values to provide for emotional engagement and a common identity. Provides the foundation for multiple cultures in explore and exploit sub-units.
- An aligned senior team with the cognitive flexibility to manage the ambidextrous form and to relentlessly communicate a consistent message about the need for ambidexterity. This requires a common reward system based on metrics for the entire business.
- An organizational architecture that includes different alignments and physical separation to explore and exploit sub-units (different business models, competencies, incentives, metrics and cultures) with targeted integration to leverage firm-wide assets and capabilities. This requires senior-level integration and lower-level tactical integration.

---

[42] Dutta, S. (2012), page 85
[43] Rf.: Dutta, S. (2012), page 86

- Ambidextrous leadership that tolerates the contradictions of multiple alignments and is able to effectively and quickly resolve the inevitable trade-offs and conflicts that occur."[44]

According to Dutta organizations should exhibit and or balance between the following 10 characteristics to nurture ambidexterity within.

Ambidextrous Characteristics
a) Organizational Separation vs. Organizational Integration
b) Characteristics of Exploitation vs. Exploration
c) Promotion of varying subcultures
d) Organizational architecture in promoting intrapreneurship
e) Multiple cultures within the same organization
f) Sensing and seizing opportunities
g) Companies able to take big bets on future businesses
h) How leveraging of existing competencies were used to build future businesses by reconfiguration the organization
i) Capabilities to compete in mature and emerging markets and
j) Exhibition continual renewal characteristics

Figure 6: Ten Characteristics to foster Ambidexterity in organisations[45]

2.5.3 Lobbyism and Acquire hiring

The idea of lobbyism with reference to dynamic capabilities is beside to adapt to a changing environment to influence the environment in a way that the firm's competences can be utilized. Lobbying capability is a high level capability that most firms have implemented in their practices as a basis for competitive advantage. It includes activities such as litigating a case in court, making campaign contributions and lobbying a legislator or regulator.[46]

Another understanding of dynamic capabilities in order to react on changing requirements is "Acqui hiring" which is the acquisition of small companies primarily to access to their employees and to contact their knowledge and data. Alternative to mergers and acquisition a company can use licencing or patents to access knowledge.[47]

---

[44] O'Reilly III, C.A. (2007), page 61
[45] Dutta, S. (2012), page 89
[46] Lawton, T, page 5-6; Lobbyism is a wide filed and can`t be pictured in detail in this assignment.
[47] Rf.: Chatterji, A. (2014), page 1

3 Analyses of the dynamic capabilities within IBM

This section presents a business research on literature basis by utilize mainly the internet to answer the question "How did IBM satisfies customer needs and what of this initiatives can be categorised as dynamic capabilities?"

As shown in section 1.3.1 IBM has undergone a dramatic transformation. In the mid-1980s IBM had a market share of 40 % in the computer industry and a profit share of 70 %. In 1990 IBM was five times as big as the second largest competitor.[48] But IBM was at its peak at that time and was caught in a crisis.[49] The stock price was as low as in 1983. The company had been nearly written off. Size and inflexibility seemed to be the reasons for losing market share. CEO John Aker tried to transform IBM but failed. In 1993 Lou Gerstner was appointed as the new CEO. He noted that the costs ran out of control, the company lost contact to its customers; the company was too decentralized and was stock to old strategies.[50] He said: "We don't move fast enough in this company. This is an industry in which success goes to the swift more than to the smart. We've got to become more nimble, entrepreneurial, focused, cost driven...we've been too bureaucratic and preoccupied with our own view of the world ..."[51]

When Lou Gerstner became the new CEO, the service unit contributes 27 % of the revenues and a software unit didn´t exit. In 2001 the software unit generated revenues of 35 billion $ (42 %) and the service unit of 13 billion $ (16 %). The market price increased sevenfold between 1993 and 2001. In 2006, software and services generated 70 % of the revenues. IBM became a Change Architect[52] and there dynamic capabilities are crucial to the strategic dimension in there Sustain Change Readiness Model. Sustained Change Readiness is the overall capability that enables Change Architects to master continuous transformation.[53] Therefore the dynamic capabilities and Sustain Change Readiness discussions are very close related.

---

[48] Rf.: Harreld, J. B. (2006), page 12
[49] Rf.: IBM Strategy (2001), page 1
[50] Rf.: Harreld, J. B. (2006), page 13
[51] Harreld, J. B. (2006), page 13
[52] Change Architect is a IBM internal term and refers to organisations with the ability to consistently drive successful project results
[53] Rf.: Rolff, B. (2015), page 7 and 15

3.1 The IBM Business Leadership Model

Until 1993 strategies were not created by the management.[54] This work was taken over by employees. Therefore strategy papers lacked of realistic assumptions and painted a too positive picture of the situation and the success of actual strategies. Such papers were merely meant to satisfy the senior management. Strategy planning meetings took place only once in a year.[55]

Therefore Lou Gerstner introduced the IBM Business Leadership Model. Essential parts of this model are a permanent strategy process and a tight link between strategy planning and execution. It emphasizes the leadership role of a general manager. The model can be graphically represented as follows:

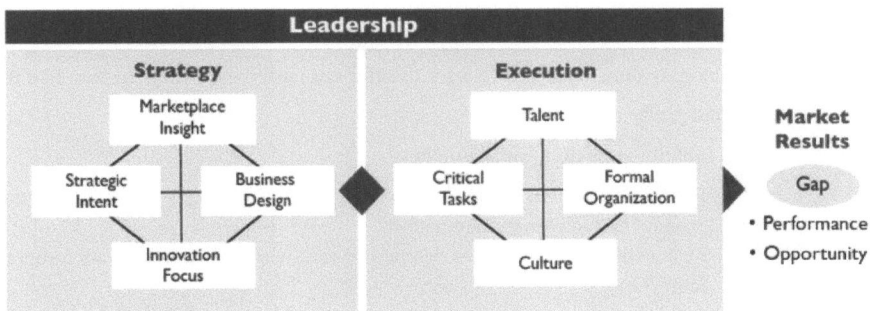

Figure 7: The IBM Business Leadership Model[56]

The starting point is dissatisfaction with a performance gap or an opportunity gap. A performance gap is a divergence between the actual and the desired performance. An opportunity gap is a divergence between the actual business results and those that were possible with a different business model. General Managers define gaps in a way as they were the business owners. That means, they quantify the gap and determine a schedule to close it. The next paragraphs of this paper are explaining the model in more detail.

---

[54] Rf.: Harreld, J. B. (2006), page 16
[55] ibid, page 16
[56] Harreld, J. B. (2006), page 35

3.1.1 Strategy

The strategy (left part of figure 7) has 4 disciplines.[57]

- Strategic Intent determines the general direction and targets the organisation aims at.
- Marketplace Insight looks at customer needs and desires, competitor's behaviour, technological and economic developments. This discipline is about fact-gathering.
- Innovation Focus requests general managers to develop a strategy with the given or available resources. It forces managers to develop their innovative thinking. This is not only about new products or services, but also about operational and business model innovation.
- Business Design is based on the 3 sub disciplines and demands answers on the following five questions:
  - Customer selection: Which customers do we want and do we not want?
  - Value proposition: What do we want to offer our customers? Why do they like the offer and prefer it?
  - Value capture: How do we make money?
    - Scope of activities: What do we do internally in order to offer a good product and to earn money with it?
    - Sustainability: How do we defend our turnover against actions of competitors?[58]

3.1.2 Execution

The developed strategy leads to a clearly communicated business design and to the provision of the needed resources. Implementation begins with an honest inventory of existing capabilities and organizational barriers. The model forces managers to compare the actual and the desired status and to undertake the efforts to reach the latter. Execution (right part of figure 7) also consists of four disciplines:

- Critical tasks and processes: These are the main activities and success factors that are necessary to pursue the chosen strategy and the concrete tasks in order to create an added value for customers.

---

[57] Rf.: Harreld, J. B. (2006), page 19
[58] ibid, page 19

- Formal organization: This discipline compares the actual and the necessary structure of the affected unit and deals with the question: does the actual structure facilitate the tasks?
- People and skills: This discipline examines the already existing employees, their skills and motivation.
- Culture: This dimension questions, what characterizes IBM's corporate culture? Does this culture support the desired business design and goals?[59]

The re-design of the strategic department was crucial for success. Such department is quite often good at formulating a strategy. But very often is not capable to implement a strategy in the existing organization. It fails in giving concrete recommendations and instructions. IBM changed the organization of the strategy department in a way that general managers switched to the strategy unit for a period of 18 to 30 months.[60] This ensures that the practical view is still considered and part of the final strategy. An academic planning culture changed to an action-oriented approach.

3.2 IBM's Dynamic capabilities

The company must be able to recognize opportunities. The strategy planning serves the abilities to sense and to seize these opportunities. Additionally it needs to have the functional ability to seize them.[61]

3.2.1 Sensing new opportunities

IBM initiated processes and organizational changes in order to sense new opportunities. These instruments and the related practices can be best expressed with table 2 below.

---

[59] ibid, page 20
[60] ibid, page 22
[61] ibid, page 23

	How often?	Members	What?	Possible outcome
Technology team	monthly	- IBM fellows - experienced engineers	- assess market readiness and potential of emerging technology	- accelerated funding for a project or its demise
Strategy team	monthly	- selected general managers - strategy executives - other key functional leaders	- examines market results of current strategies - explores new growth areas	- new market entries - adjustments to actual business plans - exit from a business
Integration and Values teams	permanently	- 300 key leaders	- integrating corporate-wide strategies	
Deep Dive	on request	- members of the affected operating unit - members of the strategy team	- structured process in order to close a performance or an opportunity gap	- change strategy - pursue strategy - exit market

Table 2: Sensing new opportunities within the IBM Business Leadership Model[62]

This set of processes and the connected way of working ensures that opportunities are identified and that necessary steps can be taken to seize them.

3.2.2 Seizing new opportunities

The capability of sensing the market, the environment and its opportunities is one thing, to be able to seizing these opportunities the other one. As former CEO Gerstner already said when he became IBM's CEO, the problem at IBM was not finding new ways of strategy but the execution. "What IBM lacked was not the ability to foresee threats and opportunities but the capability to reallocate assets and reconfigure the organization to address them." [63] The main task was to find the right way for execution and thus seizing the opportunities.

IBM not only developed diverse mechanisms that help to identify new opportunities but also those that help to seize these opportunities. The four actions designed to seize the opportunities by reallocating resources and reconfiguring the organization are Winning Plays of

---

[62] ibid, page 24
[63] Harreld, J. B. (2007), page 26

Integration & Values Team, Emerging Business Opportunities, Strategic Leadership Forums and Corporate Investment Fund. [64]

- **Integration & Values Team and Winning Plays** is described above, but this mechanism doesn't contain only elements for sensing opportunities but also some that help seizing them.
- IBM recognized that starting to operate new businesses within a mature one is difficult and that their management system did not support these new business opportunities enough. Even worse, the new businesses often got killed. Thus they developed the process of Emerging Business Opportunities. "**Emerging Business Opportunities (EBOs)** are an integrated set of processes, incentives, and structures designed explicitly to enable IBM to address new business opportunities and drive revenue growth." [65] An EBO typically begins by identifying growth opportunities for which cross-organization integration is necessary, is characterized by a new value proposition and is strongly reviewed by a senior sponsor monthly. New organizations within the company are built with their own leadership, alignment and funding. In order to receive all the resources that are necessary to explore the opportunity these new businesses are oversight by senior management. This process drives asset reallocation, which is another important factor that defines dynamic capabilities, permits the company to reconfigure itself and allows IBM to systematically experiment in new areas, whereas the rest of the company focuses on exploitation.
- The **Strategic Leadership Forum (SLFs)** is a very useful mechanism to solve major strategic problems and is used throughout IBM. It is a team-based workshop with duration of 3.5 days where important topics are discussed in disciplined conversations and sometimes also emotional debates. SLFs are usually built around a performance or opportunity gap and the purpose of the workshop is to refine the gap statement, challenging the strategy, make a root cause analysis of the gap, develop an implementation plan and also provide senior follow-up to ensure execution. For instance SLFs were used to accelerate the development of Emerging Business Opportunities, addressing performance gaps within mature businesses or even resolving significant organizational conflicts across lines of business.

---

[64] Rf.: Harreld, J. B. (2007), page 34
[65] Harreld, J. B. (2007), page 36

- The **Corporate Investment Fund** is a $500M fund that is taken from existing units in order to provide funding for new initiatives and opportunities identified by EBOs or the Integration & Values Team. The reason for this fund is that new businesses and future oriented projects often don't get enough financial support from profit-centre-managers and thus need to be protected from the normal budgetary cycle. Especially also because they arise during the year and cut across business units. This fund was used for example to support service-oriented architecture in the software group after committing on the on demand transformation or for the accelerated development of executive talent in China and India. [66]

With this Business Leadership Model and all the processes it includes, IBM emphasizes strategic insight and execution as well as general management leadership responsibility and provides an integrated set of mechanisms to sense and seize opportunities. "This allows the firm to consider trends in markets and technology, to identify issues that are relevant to customers, to examine them in detail, and to reconfigure assets to address them." [67] Hence IBM meets the most important criterion that defines dynamic capabilities and is thus a perfect example of how to bring theory into action.

3.3 Cultural change

In order to be successful a company doesn't only need to have the right strategy but also the corporate culture that matches with the company's strategy. Otherwise the culture would hinder the company's strategy. Former CEO of IBM Louis V. Gerstner, Jr. stated that IBM already had the right strategies; the question though was if the existing culture supports these strategies. As the example of one division that had been competing on technical excellence in stable markets and announced a new growth initiative that placed a premium on initiative and risk taking only to find out that the dominant culture was highly risk averse and thus required a significant shift in the culture of that unit shows, this was not the case within IBM. [68] What IBM needed concerning Gerstner was a cultural change that allowed them to reconfigure themselves and to reallocate resources that they could execute their strategies. [69]

---

[66] ibid, page 36-39
[67] ibid, page 39
[68] Rf.: Harreld, J. B. (2007), page 33
[69] ibid, page 40

Changing a culture within a company however is not easy. Usually organizations and people are not open for change and willing to do so, especially when it affects them directly. Often it is hard for people to understand why the culture they feel good and comfortable in should be changed, especially when they also had success with it. And even if they know that it must change it might be difficult for them to do it. Thus transformation begins with a sense of crisis or urgency, as Gerstner says. "No institution will go through fundamental change unless it believes it is in deep trouble and needs to do something different to survive." [70] And this is what Gerstner started to do within IBM when he arrived. What helped him in doing this was that he was an outsider and had no emotional attachment yet. The main change in the corporate culture was that teamwork counts more. Before Gerstner's arrival different divisions competed against each other and the entire company was more preoccupied with itself than with its customers. The change was to reward teamwork. Compensations of employees were measured of the performance of the whole company instead of the employee's particular division. Furthermore he wanted his employees to getting things done fast and not to studying things to death nor to chase obsessive perfectionism. This whole process of cultural transformation wouldn't be an easy and fast track, Gerstner estimated it would take five years to turn around IBM's culture; in fact it probably took even longer. [71] To integrate as a team inside the company was the right decision as IBM's success indicates. Now the culture of a common language and a problem solving methodology as manifest in the IBM Business Leadership Model is employed throughout the whole company. [72]

3.4 The success in concrete results and figures

Until the early 1990s IBM was a technology, traditional hardware company. Back in 1993 for example the services unit of IBM accounted for only 27 percent of the company's total revenues and the software unit didn't exist yet. [73] But IBM was on a massive downturn and change became necessary. IBM recognized that and Gerstner, its new CEO at that time, made the following forecast: "our bet was this: Over the next decade, customers would increasingly value companies that could provide solutions – solutions that integrated technology from various suppliers and, more importantly, integrated technology into the processes of the

---

[70] Rf.: Harvard Business School (2002)
[71] Rf.: Forbes (2002)
[72] Rf.: Harreld, J. B. (2007), page 41
[73] ibid, page 21

enterprise." [74] As described before, not only sensing new opportunities but also seizing them is important. IBM anticipated new customer value propositions to positioning itself, now the key was execution to capturing the market. Thanks to its new approach to strategy and its dynamic capabilities, IBM leveraged and reconfigured its resources and could provide the type of value desired by customers. [75] IBM was able to make the transition from a technical company to this service providing "on-demand business", which gave them a strong competitive advantage. In 2007 more than 70 percent of IBMs total revenues came from software and services. [76]

Then again IBM recognized other new trends in the fast changing and developing IT market. Global integration, new computing models, new client needs for integration and innovation and a massive amount of data transformed the industry and the global economy. IBM adapted fast and transformed itself to change their business mix to higher value, more profitable technologies and market opportunities. Growth Markets, Cloud, Business Analytics and Smarter Planet became the key fields from which IBM draws big revenues. What helped IBM to accelerate this transformation were strategic sales, merger and acquisitions. Since 2000 IBM has been acquiring more than 140 companies in different areas such as analytics, cloud or smarter commerce. [77] The latest deals were partnerships with Apple, SAP and Tencent and a strategic alliance with Twitter. IBM not only grew new businesses through acquisitions but also organically and by reinventing business continually. [78] IBM still continues to come up with more innovations than any other company year after year.

Due to this transformation from a pure hardware company to a high value innovation, service and software company pretax income of IBM grow steadily over the years and the product scope changed continuously, as figure 8 shows.

---

[74] ibid, page 26
[75] Rf.: Urbany J. E. (2010), page 168
[76] Rf.: Harreld, J. B. (2007), page 21
[77] Rf.: Generating Higher Value at IBM (2012), page 2
[78] Rf.: IBM Annual Report (2014), page 3-4

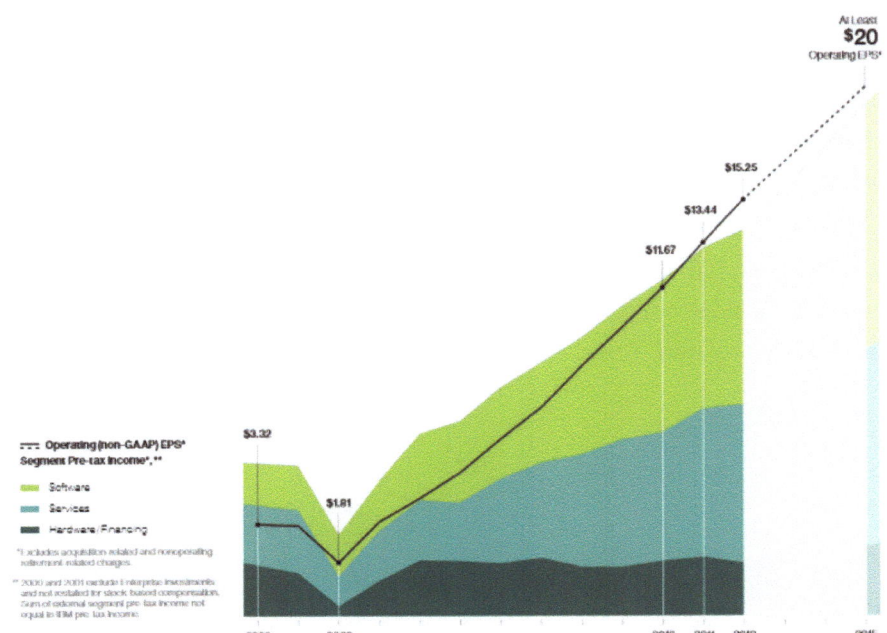

Figure 8: IBM Segment pretax income[79]

"In 2000, for example, hardware and financing accounted for 35% of income, services for 40% and software for 25%. In 2006 this percentages shifted to 23% in hardware and financing and 37% and 40% in services and software respectively." [80] "In 2012 the percentage of hardware and financing went back to 14%, services accounted for 41% and software for 45% of pretax income." [81]

As already mentioned, the software sector became more and more important whereas the hardware unit accounted for less percentage of IBMs income year after year. The service sector increased pretax income in real figures but remained pretty stable in percentage. IBMs estimates that in 2015 the software sector will account for at least 50% of the total income before taxes.

---

[79] ibid, page 3
[80] ibid, page 1
[81] ibid, page 1

Today the hardware unit of IBM accounts for only 10% of IBMs total revenues (as of 2014).[82] "The company's strategic imperatives are Together, cloud, analytics, mobile, social and security, which represented alone 27% of IBMs revenues. IBM works in a variety of different industries such as banking, insurance, healthcare, automotive, energy, etc. and in a large part with most of the industries leaders."[83]

As IBMs current CEO, Virginia M. Rometty, says: "IBM lives at the intersection of technology and business. This enables us to change the way the world works, and in so doing, to be essential to our clients and to society."[84] In order to "change the world" one has to be able to adapt to fast change itself. Thanks to its dynamic capabilities, IBM is able to do that.

---

[82] Rf.: IBM Annual Report (2014), page 33
[83] ibid, page 8
[84] IBM Annual Report (2014), page 8

4 Conclusion

The literature research disclosed a huge number of highly theoretical discussions whit a lack of practical approaches, methods, techniques or best practices (except IBM). This paper seems to be the first of its kind, which brings the different theories into a cohesive whole and pictures there application on a real company.

The collection, interpretation and analysis of data according to epistemological convictions have clearly showed that the extended utilisation of dynamic capabilities were crucial for the success of IBM in the recent years. The investigation of the practical case confirms the theories itemized in this document.

4.1 Relationship to organisational variables

The practice of the IBM Business Leadership Model (Section 3.1) is underlining and approving the theory regarding the relationship to organisational variables (Section 2.4).

- Market dynamism: As described, the model generally tackles the changes coming from the dynamic IT market.
- With regard to the strategy dimension it can be stated that IBM developed particular capabilities as dictated by the firm's overall business strategy. These are for example innovativeness (global leader for innovations, see section 1.3.1), experts for commodity server business, business intelligence, data analytics, business continuity, security, cloud computing, virtualization and green solutions (section 1.3).
- Only the theoretical aspect of long term performance; "dynamic capabilities are more likely to lead to better firm performance when particular capabilities are developed in line with the firm's strategic choice."[85] Can't be fully confirmed with the data available. This field should be an object of future investigations.

---

[85] Wang, C. (2007), page 24

4.2 The three main aspects of dynamic capabilities

In the passage IBM's Dynamic Capabilities (Section 3.2) the three main aspects (adaptive, absorptive and innovative) form Section 2.3 can be easily recognised. IBM developed several mechanisms and instruments that help them to meet these three aspects. Strategy teams examine markets and explore and identify emerging market opportunities. Technology teams assess the potential of new technologies and the markets readiness for it. Both these teams meet monthly what enables them to react and adapt quickly. These are adaptive and absorptive capabilities. Further IBM has a strong R&D program and invests heavily in it which brings first-hand knowledge of new technology. In addition IBM also generates knowhow from outside by partnerships or acquisitions, which provides other absorptive capabilities. All together these practices had turned into a lot of new innovation. That confirms the fact that IBM is the global leader for innovations for the 22nd consecutive year and shows IBM's innovative capabilities.

4.3 Organisational Ambidexterity

In September of 1999, Lou Gerstner, then CEO of IBM, was incensed after reading a monthly report, which indicated that current financial pressures had forced a business unit to discontinue funding of a promising new initiative. After a detailed analysis of the reasons why IBM had failed to take advantage of the opportunity and the discussions it generated among senior management, a series of recommendations were made to permit the company to succeed at both exploitation in mature markets and exploration in growth areas.[86]

These decisions resulted in the development of the Emerging Business Opportunities (EBO) initiative in 2000. Between 2000 and 2005, EBOs added $15.2B to IBM's top line. While acquisitions over this period added 9 percent to IBM's top line, EBOs added 19 percent. This process has enabled the company to explore and exploit, to both enter new businesses and to remain competitive in mature ones.[87]

---

[86] Rf.: Stanford Business, WP No. 2025, page 19
[87] ibid, page 21

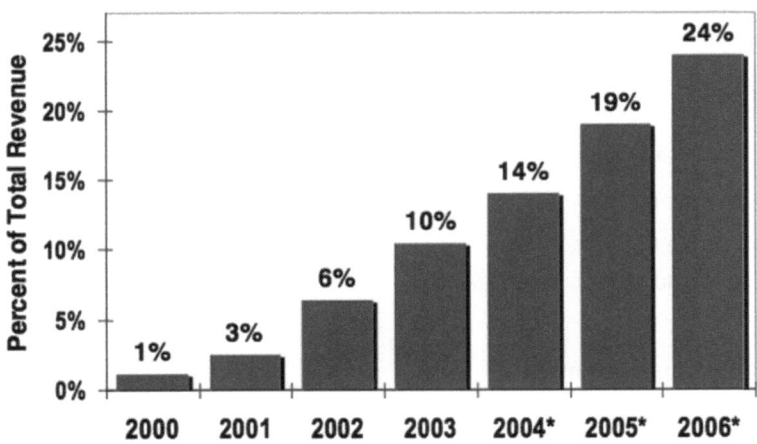

Figure 9: EBO Revenue as a Percent of Total IBM Revenue[88]

Organizational ambidexterity, or the dynamic capability of an organization to simultaneously explore and exploit, can be seen in the EBO process at IBM, in which new business units are systematically created, tested, and either grown or killed. Hence the theory described in section 2.5.2 can be approved.

4.4 Promoting Entrepreneurship

IBM promotes entrepreneurship on different levels. Market Insight as part of the IBM Business Leadership Model challenges managers to understand costumer's desire and the market environment (see section 3.1.1). Innovation focus on the other hand, invites managers to experiment with new ideas and to foster creative thinking (see section 3.1.1). This part of the model shall lead to new products and services as well as to new production and operational processes. IBM also installed teams with different tasks (see section 3.2.1). The technology team examines the potential of new technologies and assesses the market readiness. The strategy team is a high-calibre team that explores new growth areas amongst other things. Entrepreneurship is also fostered by organisational changes. The strategy department, for example, became pervious (see section 3.1.2) to avoid tunnel vision and to allow new visions on a workable basis.

---

[88] ibid, page 39

4.5 Lobbyism and Acquire hiring

Only for Lobbyism no evidences have been found or pictured in this assignment. Even it is likely that a big enterprise like IBM attempts this activity. Thus this is also an interesting field of future research.

Despite the fact that IBM acquired since 2000 more than 140 companies in different areas (see section 3.4) there is no other evidence or data for "Acquire hiring" pictured. So it is also a motivating field for forthcoming studies.

4.6 Recommendation

To follow up on this scientific question "How IBM did satisfies customer needs and what of this initiatives can be categorised as dynamic capabilities?" the authors would suggest to investigate on the following scientific fields.

- As mentioned in the previous paragraph, the theoretical aspect of long term performance can't be fully confirmed with the data available. Therefore future studies could try to quantitatively confirm that dynamic capabilities enhance long term performance or asking "What specific dynamic capabilities can enhance or secure long term performance of a company?" This would completely approve or partly put into question the theory of Wang (2007).
- Also above, Lobbyism and Acquire hiring can be an item of future studies. It could be asked "How Lobbyism can interplay with dynamic capabilities in a specific industry?" or "To what extend the Acquisitions of IBM where supportive for their dynamic capabilities?"
- Furthermore the question "How does IBM promote entrepreneurship in there organisation?" or in general "What are technics to foster entrepreneurship within a big company in order to enhance dynamic capability?" might be of importance for the scientific field of strategic management.

List of appendices

Appendix 1: ITM Checklist

List of references

Cloud Computing (2015): IBM Sets It Eyes On The Cloud, from: Management Journal, March/April, page 11

Dutta, S. (2012): Dynamic Capabilities Fostering Ambidexterity, from: SCMS Journal of Indian Management, April-June, Ahmedabad, 2012, page 83

O'Reilly III, C.A./Tushman, M.L. (2007): Ambidexterity as a Dynamic Capability: Resolving the Innovator's Dilemma, Working paper from Graduate School of Business Stanford University Stanford and Harvard Business School Boston, 2007

Dahm, M. H./Haindl, C. (2007) Strategisches Management im Wandel der Zeit, from: ZUb–Zeitschrift der Unternehmensberatung, 1(07), 15-24

Hutterer, P. (2013): Dynamic Capabilities und Innovationsstrategien, 1st Edition, Wiesbaden

Rieser, M. (2014): Dynamic Capability und organisationale Kompetenz, 1st Edition, Wiesbaden

Amberg, M./Bodendorf, F./Möslein, K. (2010): Wertschöpfungsorientierte

Dinsmore, P.C./ Canabis-Brewin, J. (2006): AMA Handbook of Project Management, 2nd Edition, USA

Chatterji, A./Patro, A. (2014): DYNAMIC CAPABILITIES AND MANAGING HUMAN CAPITAL, from: The Academy of Management Perspectives 2014, Vol. 28, No. 4, Durham 2014, pages 395-408

Wang, C./Ahmed, P. (2007): Dynamic Capabilities: A Review and Research Agenda, from: The International Journal of Management Reviews, 9(1), Middlesex, 2007, page 31-51

Ambrosini, V./ Bowman, C. / Collier, N. (2009): Dynamic capabilities: An exploration of how firms renew their resource base, from: British Journal of Management, vol. 20, no. S1, Cardiff, 2009, pages 9-24

Protogerou, A./Caloghirou, Y./Lioukas, S. (2011): Dynamic capabilities and their indirect impact on firm performance, from: Industrial and Corporate Change, Volume 21, Number 3, Oxford, 2011, pages 615–647

Lawton, T./Rajwani, T.: DESIGNING LOBBYING CAPABILITIES: MANAGERIAL CHOICES IN UNPREDICTABLE ENVIRONMENTS, from: European Business Review, Volume 23, Issue 2, Bedfordshire, 2007, pages 167-189

Harreld, J.B./O Reilly, C.A./Tushman, M.L.(2007): Dynamic Capabilities at IBM: Driving Strategy into Action, from: California Management Review, Volume 4, No. 4, Berkeley, 2007, pages 21-43

Urbany, J.E./Davis J.H. (2010): Grow by Focusing on What Matters: Competitive Strategy in 3 Circles (Strategic Management Collection), Business Expert Publishing 2010

Rolff, B./ Goebel, E. (2015): Sustained Change Readiness -For Continuous Enterprise Transformation-, Presentation and Discussion Paper, Mai/2015, FOM MBA Strategic Corporate Management Module Guest Lecture, Hamburg.

Harreld, J.B./O'Reilly, C.A./Tushman, M.L.(2007): Dynamic Capabilities at IBM: Driving Strategy into Action, 2006

List of internet references

Ken Blanchard (2010): "Mastering the Art of Change", page 44:
URL: http://www.kenblanchard.com/img/pub/blanchard_mastering_the_art_of_change.pdf

(23.04.2015)
Zeepedia (2015): "Change Management":
URL:http://www.zeepedia.com/read.php?benefits_and_significance_of_change_management_change_management&b=29&c=2 (23.04.2015)

Chron (2015): "Change in Organizations":
URL: http://smallbusiness.chron.com/change-important-organization-728.html (23.04.2015)

Everydaylife (2015): Globalpost "Importance of Change in an Organization":
URL: http://everydaylife.globalpost.com/importance-change-organization-4297.html (23.04.2015)

The Atlantic (2011): "IBM`s 100 Years":
URL: http://www.theatlantic.com/technology/archive/2011/06/ibms-first-100-years-a-heavily-illustrated-timeline/240502/ (23.04.2015)

IBM Annual Report (2008):
URL: ftp://ftp.software.ibm.com/annualreport/2008/2008_ibm_annual.pdf#page=12 (23.04.2015)

IBM Annual Report (2014):
URL: http://www.ibm.com/annualreport/2014/bin/assets/IBM-Annual-Report-2014.pdf (23.04.2015)

WSJ (2015): Wall Street Journal "IBM Continue Painful Transition"
URL: http://www.wsj.com/articles/ibm-reports-another-revenue-decline-1429561027 (23.04.2015)

247wall (2015): "The Worlds Most Innovative Companies":
URL: http://247wallst.com/special-report/2015/01/13/the-worlds-most-innovative-companies/ (23.04.2015)

Forbes (2014): "Powerful Brands":
URL: http://www.forbes.com/powerful-brands/list/ (23.04.2015)

Finance Yahoo (2015): "Buffet remains confident in IBMs business prospects":

URL: http://finance.yahoo.com/news/buffett-remains-confident-ibms-business-111016880.html (05.05.2015)

IBM Strategy (2001): New Models For the Future
URL: http://www-03.ibm.com/ibm/history/documents/pdf/strategy.pdf (13.05.2015)

Stanford Business (2009): „Organizational Ambidexterity: IBM and Emerging Business Opportunities", WP No. 2025
URL: https://www.gsb.stanford.edu/faculty-research/working-papers/organizational-ambidexterity-ibm-emerging-business-opportunities (21.05.2015)

Generating Higher Value at IBM (2012):
URL: http://www.ibm.com/investor/att/pdf/2012_ibm_higher_value.pdf (22.05.2015)

Generating Higher Value at IBM (2006):
URL: http://www.ibm.com/investor/att/pdf/2006_ibm_higher_value.pdf (22.05.2015)

Forbes (2002): "How Lou Gerstner Got IBM To Dance"
URL: http://www.forbes.com/2002/11/11/cx_ld_1112gerstner.html (14.05.2015)

Harvard Business School (2002): "Gerstner: Changing Culture at IBM - Lou Gerstner Discusses Changing the Culture at IBM"
URL: http://hbswk.hbs.edu/archive/3209.html (14.05.2015)

Appendix 1: ITM Checklist

Topics	Issues critical to success	Comments / suggestions
General economics	Economic relevance of the topic	In the economics area, strategic management and the intersection of dynamic capabilities and especially the innovative capabilities of companies are the motor for economic growth and is therefore of huge relevance. Innovation leads to technical development and consequently to economic growth, enhanced convenience in live and better living standards.
Strategic management	Relevance of the topic concerning - Securing existence - Competitive advantages - Tying up resources - Sustainability - Risk	As described in the assignment, dynamic capabilities are beyond securing existence, develop a competitive advantage and defend it, tying up resources and doing risk management. Nonetheless dynamic capabilities are considering these aspects to secure sustainability. As dynamic capabilities itself is a discussion in the field of strategic management the relevance to it is high.
Marketing	Advantages and disadvantages from the proposition regarding - marketing measures - external impact - general productivity - internal/external marketing	Marketing must be an important aspect for dynamic capabilities and there related innovation. The Marketing department of a company can give input (external impact). It the sense that is knows best what customers want and subsequently can inspire R&D to bring innovative products or services. Additionally marketing uses his marketing technics (6P, internal/external marketing...) to create demand at the customer and bring the product to the market and increase sales. This is to say, if there is an improper marketing even the best innovation won´t sale and the R&D efficiency of the company would be recognized as low.
Financial management	When choosing appropriate terms of financing - criteria's that have to be considered - risks and safeguarding measures - impact of externalities	The decision on a market entry or exit has significant financial implications. This assignment shows exemplary processes to minimize this risk. Innovations can result in obvious or hidden externalities. Taking the electro car, which technically enhances the use of nuclear energy? The resulting financial risks need to be considered as well not just on company but also on general economy and political level.

Human resources management	Personal consequences	The connection to the HR function comes via the related project management for innovation projects and there related personal consequences. Typical HR management tools and methods are: stuffing management plan, resource calendars, team building, team performance assessment, project performance appraisals, issue log book, responsibility assignment matrix, resource-breakdown structure and resource histograms. Using this PM tools properly will help to secure project success and consequently enhances R&D efficiency as well as the dynamic capabilities.
Business law	- legal topics - steps to ensure legal certainty	Innovations can have internal (personal) and external (environmental) legal consequences. These consequences are needed to be within the frame of law and assessed according to their legal impact. Also patents, property rights and certifications need to be considered.
Research methods / management decision making	- sources of information to be practiced in order to stay up-to-date - decision criteria to be practiced on the choice of alternatives	Research methods are utilized and shown in this assignment (technology team, strategy team, integration and value teams, deep dive-process) As this assignment is showing real live circumstances. It can be acknowledge as a business research. All conclusions derived from the entire dynamic capability framework should be made according to epistemological convictions.
Soft skills / leadership qualities	- managerial requirements for implementation - forms of reasonable leadership behavior	The resulting innovations need to be pushed and integrated by initiating several projects. This requires a project leader/team with sound project management skill to plan, manage and implement. Since R&D projects are uncertain a collaborative leadership style should be preferred. Also leadership qualities such as conflict solving abilities, listening skills, decision making, integrative thinking, data and information management and on a of essence.